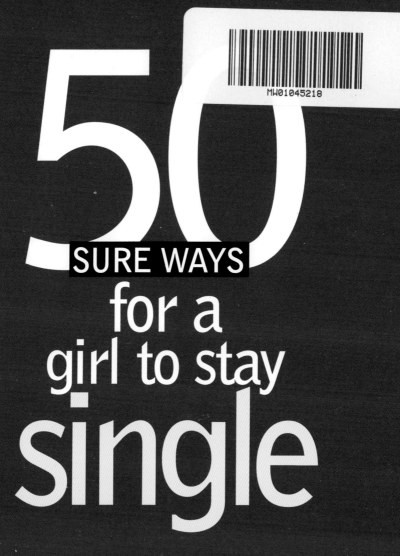

50

SURE WAYS

for a
girl to stay
single

50

SURE WAYS

for a
girl to stay

single

**Written and illustrated
by Pim Pauline Øvergaard**

**Andrews McMeel
Publishing**

Kansas City

ISBN: 0-7407-4712-6

Library of Congress Control Number: 2004102778

04 05 06 07 08 KF04
 10 9 8 7 6 5 4 3 2 1

50

SURE WAYS

for a
girl to stay

single

1

Use baby talk as often as possible!

2

Start every sentence with *I, me,* or *my!*

3

Make a big deal out of everything . . .

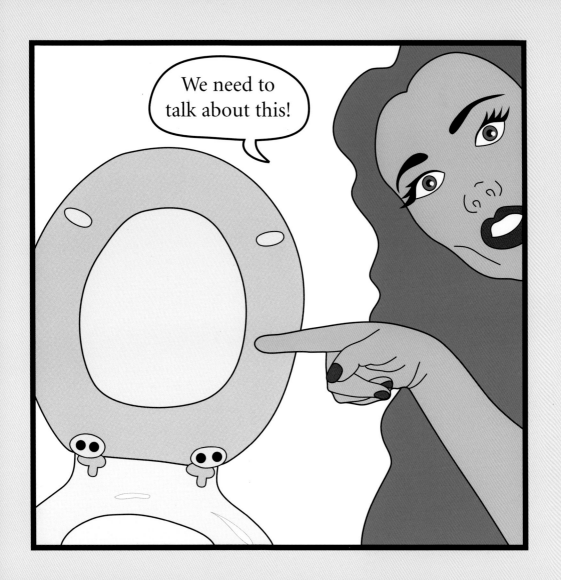

4

. . . unless it's his issue!

5

Always count calories!

6

Keep staring at his "package" and then sigh repeatedly as if disappointed!

7

Always put men down!

8

Make a list of things he has to change about his appearance and behavior before he can be with you!

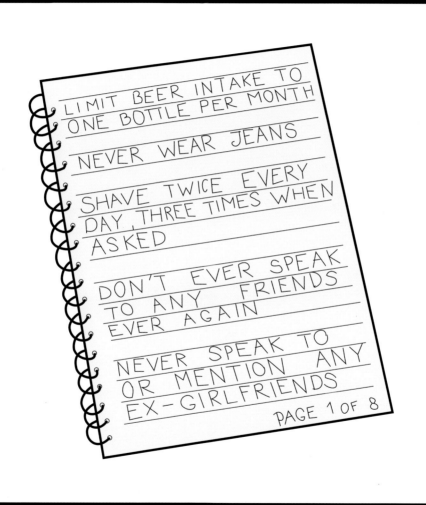

9

Chain-smoke!

10

Tell him you love him on your first date!

11

Send several bouquets of flowers to his workplace the day after your first date.

12

Tell him about your recurring depressions
and the different ways you tried to
kill yourself. Make some up if necessary.

13

Use "I don't know" as
an answer for everything!

14

Only invite him over if
your house is a mess!

15

Always leave some hints around
to show your true intentions!

16

Let him know you live only for him!

17

Give him a detailed description
of the sex dream you had
about his best friend!

18

Never shave!

19

Complain to the waiter about everything,
have him take it back, but change
your mind when he returns!

20

Tell him you once tried to kill your ex, then start to laugh hysterically!

21

Tape over his porn with
Touched by an Angel!

22

Never laugh at his jokes!

23

Shout out some other guy's name in bed!

24

Ask him if he goes to therapy and then, whatever the answer, give him a list of therapists you recommend!

25

Make long-term plans on your first date!

26

Order three desserts and tell him
how nice it is not having to worry
about your appearance now that
you've "found" him.

27

Arrange for him to pick you up somewhere and make him wait for at least an hour. Make sure not to apologize.

28

Be confrontational at any given moment
and argue with everything he says.

29

Flirt openly with the bartender and make sure you get his phone number!

30

Point out his flaws.
If he doesn't have any, make some up.

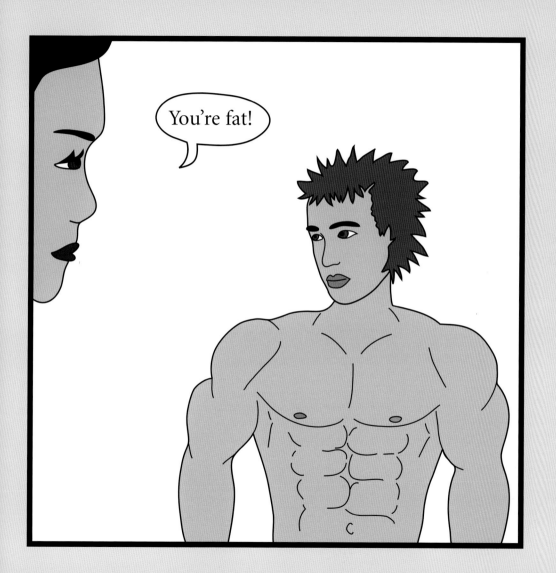

31

Flirt with his friends!

32

Never even try to pay the bill!

33

Bring up your ex as often as possible!

34

Tell him about your extreme credit card debt and how you're just waiting for the "right man" to pay it off!

35

Give him a detailed description of everything
you bought on your shopping spree!

36

Call him several times every day,
and then be quiet and wait for him to talk.

37

Always wear more than one
layer of makeup!

38

Reapply your lipstick at least
every ten minutes!

39

Chew with your mouth open!

40

Use *we* as often as possible!

41

Party all night before your date.
Don't shower or brush your teeth!

42

Bring a book of baby names to your first date and circle the ones you like with a pink marker!

43

Start to cry after your first kiss!

44

Live for Publicly Displayed Affection!

45

Take every opportunity to
check out your own reflection!

46

Always be ready for a fake headache!

47

Always show your disappointment
if he cancels.

48

Let him know you're more important than anything or anyone and make him feel guilty if you ever notice otherwise!

49

Always get drunk, fall asleep,
and throw up if possible!

50

Never leave him alone!